RADSPORTS GUIDES

SURFING

TRACY NELSON MAURER

Rourke

Publishing LLC

Vero Beach, Florida 32964

www.rourkepublishing.com

Photo Credits: Cover, p. 44: © Jeff Gross/Allsport; p. 4: © Vince Catacio/Allsport; p. 7: © USPS; p. 11: © Corbis Images; p. 13, 43: © Pierce Tostee/Allsport; p. 15, 29: © CSL; p. 117: © Mike Hewitt/Allsport; p. 20: © Jamie Squire; p. 24, 37, 40: © Allsport ; p. 27: © Corbis Images; p. 33: © Jeff Gross/Pierce Tostee/Allsport; p. 34, 35: © Christopher Ruppel/Allsport; p. 36: © Corbis Images; p. 38: © Donald Miralle/Allsport; p.28 Pierce Tostee/Getty Images

Cover photo: All over the world, people catch the waves just for fun!

The author extends appreciation to Mike Maurer and Kendall and Lois M. Nelson.

Editor: Frank Sloan

Cover and page design: Nicola Stratford

Library of Congress Cataloging-in-Publication Data

Maurer, Tracy, 1965-
  Surfing / Tracy Nelson Maurer.
     p. cm. — (Radsports guides)
Summary: Surveys the history, equipment, techniques, and safety factors
of surfing, including bodyboarding, flowboarding, and freesurfing.
Includes bibliographical references (p.   ) and index.
  ISBN 1-58952-280-X (hardcover)
  1. Surfing—Juvenile literature. 2. Extreme sports—Juvenile
literature. [1. Surfing. 2. Extreme sports.] 1. Title.
  GV840.S8 M35 2002
  797.3'2—dc21
                                              2002008226

Printed in the USA

CG/CG

TABLE OF CONTENTS

At Hawaii's Banzai Pipeline, swells from 2,000 miles (3,218 km) back push up a wall of spinning water that rolls down onto razor-sharp coral just 100 feet (30.48 m) from the sandy beach.

PLANK RIDERS

Surfing reigns as the Big Kahuna of all extreme sports. Nobody knows exactly when surfing began, but the **Polynesians** probably invented canoe surfing around 2000 BC. Hawaiians turned wave sliding, or *he`e nalu* in old Hawaiian, into an all-village sport at least a thousand years ago.

Back then, Hawaiian boys and girls rode bodyboards less than 4 feet (1.22 m) long. Adults ripped on wooden longboards that sometimes measured taller than 18 feet (5.49 m) and weighed over 150 pounds (68 kg). You needed major strength, guts, and skill to surf.

You need all of that today, plus a swimsuit. Early surfers rode nude—talk about extreme!

chapter

ONE

LONG ON HISTORY

Long ago, people around the world surfed simply because they liked to play in the waves. In the 1700s, European explorers wrote about wave-sliding Hawaiians. A century later, European sailors wrote about kids bodysurfing near the coasts of Peru and western Africa.

The Europeans frowned on this fun in the sun. The sport began to die out by the 1900s.

Thankfully, a few dedicated geezers on the Hawaiian Islands kept paddling out to catch a wave once in a while. They handed down what they knew to a few curious kids who didn't care that surfing was old-fashioned.

EXTREME ATTITUDE

When Hawaii joined the United States in 1959, surfing had already reached California's shores. American surfers kept the Hawaiian spirit alive there by guarding the sport against too much hype. Surfers' anti-fashion attitude helped surfing develop its own culture.

Even when Dick Dale, The Bel Airs, and The Beach Boys tuned America's teenagers to "surf music," and Hollywood cranked out kissy surfer movies, the true surfers stayed focused. They didn't put up with **posers** or spasts, those fakey people who think pricey equipment replaces skill.

Surfing's attitude is still the soul of all extreme sports today. It's about pushing yourself faster and higher. You polish your sessions with control and style for nobody's show but your own. In your head, you always check the danger levels and maintain safety. Risk wisely. Rip it finely.

USA 34

DUKE KAHANAMOKU

2002

In 2002, the U.S. Postal Service released a stamp with Hawaiian Duke Paoa Kahanamoku's image on it. Duke helped keep surfing alive in the early 1900s. Many people call him the father of modern big-wave surfing.

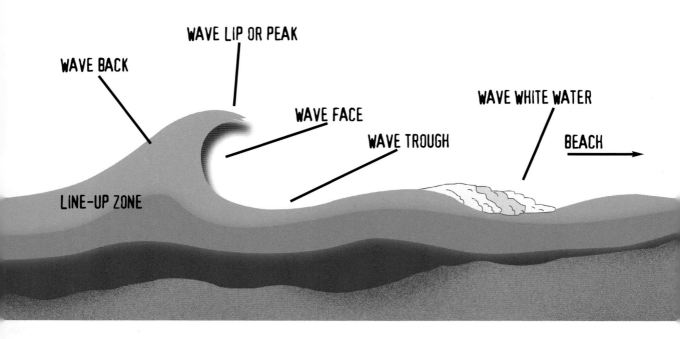

WAVE BACK

WAVE LIP OR PEAK

WAVE FACE

WAVE TROUGH

WAVE WHITE WATER

BEACH

LINE-UP ZONE

WAVE ON

Before you try surfing or other ocean sports, learn to swim well. You should be able to swim at least half of a football field without stopping or gasping for air.

Check the weather forecast, tide times, and wind speed before you hit the beach. Ask the lifeguard for the latest conditions.

Always take time to study the waves. Judge wave size from **trough** to crest. For every foot of wave height, study the waves for two to three minutes. That means watching five-footers for a good ten to fifteen minutes.

Count the number of waves in a set. Note the time between sets, or the period. A 12-second period usually means some good waves, called ground swells. Anything less than ten seconds probably means wind swells, those sloppy waves churned by local wind. Surfers try to paddle out between sets.

IF IN DOUBT, JUST STAY OUT!

Most lifeguards post warnings during high surf conditions. Don't go into the ocean if you're not a strong, experienced swimmer. In some places, high surf means wave heights over 25 feet (7.62 m)!

Some beaches also post **riptide** warnings. A normal rip current, or run out, feels freaky because the waves suck you out to sea.

Stay calm if you get caught in a rip current. Tired surfers can drown. Paddle parallel to the shore, not toward shore.

Hazard Check
Scan the area for rocks, jetties, or other hazards. Ask the lifeguard to point them out. Plan where you'll paddle in. Plan where to swim out if you bail.

SMOOTH MOVE

Practice dry first. Lie flat on the ground. Let only your chest, stomach, and knees touch the ground. Make sure your feet stay in the air. Then hold your arms straight out from your sides, not letting them touch the ground. Tilt your head up so you can look straight ahead. Hold this position. Balancing on the board feels like th s.

PLAN YOUR STANCE

Your **stance**, or position on the board, should feel comfortable, balanced, and controlled. Are you a regular foot (left foot forward) or a goofy foot (right foot forward)? Skateboarders or snowboarders usually use the same foot forward on a surfboard.

From your balance position on the ground, practice jumping up. Place your hands 24 to 28 inches (61 to 71 cm) apart, about where you would for a push-up.

Always place your front foot down first, tucked under your chest. That front knee stays bent. Your back leg stays out with a loose knee. Don't kneel (kneeling is dweeby).

Push up into a crouch. Bend those knees! Aim your toes at one side of the surfboard. Point your shoulders forward with your hands by your hips, ready to add balance.

RAD TIP

Is Your Best Foot Forward?
Try this test. Run, then slide in your socks, across a wooden floor. Which foot goes forward? Put the same foot forward on your surfboard.

Always keep your knees bent and your arms out for balance.

MANNERS MATTER

Surfers made their own rules a long time ago. Before you join the crew at the line-up—the waiting area just ahead of where the waves break—watch the order.

- An upright rider closest to the wave break has the right of way. He or she claims it by whistling or yelling.
- "Snaking a wave" or cutting in front of another rider on his or her claimed wave is hugely rude. Nobody likes a tailgater, either. One surfer on one wave is your best policy.
- Don't make anyone dodge you; stay out of the way, even if you get smashed by the whitewater.
- Apologize if you screw up.

Mostly, use common courtesy and you won't steam anyone.

BOARD BASICS

Surfing is part art and part science. Every session is a **physics** lesson. The Swiss scientist Daniel Bernoulli, who probably never surfed, came up with Bernoulli's Principles in the 1700s. They still apply.

Water hits the nose of the board and chokes as you tap into the wave's **momentum**. The liquid smooths out and rushes under the middle of the board. You gain speed there. Then the water meets at the tail where it gags again. Pressure from your back foot helps control your board and prevent a wipeout.

Shapers, or board designers, use Bernoulli's Principles to create the right ride. Precise to a thirty-second of an inch, each board must balance flotation, or **buoyancy**, with performance. It's not easy.

chapter

TWO

BOARD GROUPS

Your skill, typical wave size, and surf conditions help decide which board to ride. Personal preference counts most. Board designs can use one fin, called a single fin. Some boards use two, known as a twin fin. Other designs might use three or even four fins. Each fin set-up works better with a certain kind of tail and board length.

You'll find boards with square tails and pin tails; some with double-pointed swallow tails and some with rounded squash tails. The tail's upward arc is called the rocker. More rocker delivers smoother turns, but less speed.

Shortboard
A lightweight, narrow board that often features a pointed nose and three fins.
Length: From 5' up to 7'6" (1.5 to 2.28 m)
Width: From 18" to 19-1/4" (45.7 to 48.9 cm)
Downside: Unstable for adult beginners; a poor floater that's not easy to paddle.
Upside: Good starter board for kids; excellent performance in contests for adults.
Conditions: Handles well in good-size waves.

Fun Shape
Mid-sized board with a shortboard shape and longboard stability. Similarly, a hybrid board from 7' to 9' (2.13 to 2.74 m) long also blends shortboard and longboard characteristics.
Length: From 6'10" up to 8'6" (2.08 to 2.59 m)
Width: From 21" to 22" (53.3 to 55.9 cm)
Downside: Performance lags, especially for tricks.
Upside: Easy for anyone to learn on, even in whitewater soup.
Conditions: Rips best in small to medium waves.

Choose a board that fits your skill level and the surf conditions you ride most often.

Longboard
Also called a tanker (or a mal outside the U.S.), this stocky board usually measures more than 2-1/2" (6.35 cm) thick so it floats well; it's stable and easy to maneuver.
Length: Over 9 feet (2.74 m)
Width: Usually more than 22" (55.9 cm)
Downside: Not steady in steep waves; heavy and awkward to carry.
Upside: Easy to learn on; it paddles well and catches even tiny waves.
Conditions: Dependable in most any small to medium wave.

Fast Fix
You can patch some small surface dings and cracks with a ding repair kit. Do your fix-ups right away to keep water out of the foam core.

STICKS AND SPONGES

Stand-up surfers ride sticks, or surfboards. Another type of board, called a bodyboard or boogie board, showed up in the 1970s and stayed. Foam construction earned these easy-to-ride boards the nickname "sponges." Sponges are smaller, lighter, and softer than normal surfboards.

Like surfboards, bodyboards come in all shapes and sizes. Your board should come up to your belly button.

Shapers use many different kinds of foam material today. Some foams flex more than others; some cost more than others. Beginners usually like more flex at a low cost. Better riders want a stiffer board to throw tricks, and they're willing to pay more for advanced construction.

Use your hips to press the tail for a right or left turn.

TUMMY TURNERS

Bodyboarders usually ride on their stomachs. It's harder than it looks! Tuck the board so that the tail is even with your hips. Grab the top corners and hold your elbows on the board. Keep your head up and your feet down under the water. Most spongers use flippers for extra power.

Spongers check the wave and weather conditions like surfers. They also follow the same rules. No rude dudes!

Start with small waves. As your wave starts to break, press the nose down and kick hard to catch it. To turn, use your hip to press the tail to the right or left. If you turn right, hold the right corner and use your left arm in the air for control. Turn left by switching hip pressure and hand positions. Slide forward to trim, or gain speed.

LOOKS AREN'T EVERYTHING

Graphics spiff up a board, but looks aren't everything. Before you sink money into a new board, shop around. Test many different shapes and styles. No two boards feel exactly the same. Wait to buy until you know what fits your style and size the best.

Most teen-age wannabes start surfing with a longboard. If you're a smaller person, you might like a board in the 7' to 9' range (2.13 to 2.74 m) or an egg-shaped funboard.

Try to find a cheap, used board. Check the surf shops and classified ads. If you borrow one, remember that beginners put serious wear on a board.

Buying a used board isn't rocket science. Look at the top of the board, or the deck. If it's bubbled or split, don't buy it. Make sure you have a plug for a leash. Flip the board over and check the fins. Avoid a board with major dings in the finish.

PAD YOUR DECK

You might want traction pads on the deck. Find a pad set that fits your board and looks cool. Trace the traction pads on your board where you think you want them. Put the board down and try the position. Follow the instructions or the pad won't stay stuck.

Most surfers don't wait long enough after they stick the pads on. Let the pads sit 12 to 24 hours. Using a blow dryer doesn't help. If an edge starts to peel, fix it right away with a super-glue. You don't need to wax the pads.

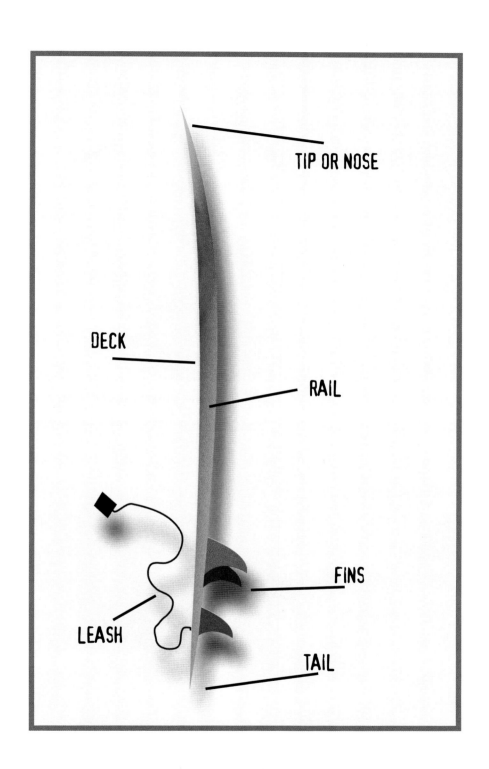

TIP OR NOSE

DECK

RAIL

FINS

LEASH

TAIL

A rash guard protects your skin from the board's rough surface.

Wetsuits work well for cool temperatures.

HOT WATER-WEAR

What's hot for styles and colors changes all the time. Real surfers care more about how the clothing works than how it looks. Surfers bang against the rough, sandy bottom. Sometimes they dump into coral or rocks. The sun's ultraviolet rays and the salt water destroy wimpy swimsuits.

Look for a comfortable but durable swimsuit that won't fall off in the surf. You might wear boardshorts, surf trunks, baggies, or jams. Each style varies in fit and performance.

In summer, a long-sleeve or short-sleeve rash guard protects your stomach and chest from the deck's wax and helps prevent sunburns. In the winter, a rash guard can be worn underneath your wetsuit to protect you from suit rash.

FEEL WARM ALL OVER

Serious surfers invest in a variety of **neoprene** wetsuits. They wear lightweight spring suits or shorties to keep warm during cool spring and fall weather. When winter comes they break out a thicker, full-length suit. Each suit can cost from $100 to $500 or more.

Choose the wetsuit style and thickness that matches the water temperature. If you surf frigid northern waters, you want a full-length hooded suit in the thickest neoprene you can find, probably 5 millimeters. Buy booties and gloves, too.

Remember to rinse your wetsuit with fresh water after every session. Hang it to dry, out of the sun. And, for Pete's sake, don't pee in it! You'll ruin the neoprene and stink like a dog.

WAX FACTS

Wax makes the deck sticky, so you don't slip off. You use different wax for warm, cool, or frigid water. Some surfers apply the wax with circular patterns for extra grip bumps. Others pull long, even strokes down the full board.

A wax comb roughs up the surface for added **traction** when you're running low. You can also use the wax comb to strip old wax before you lay down a fresh coat. Leave the board in the sun for five minutes and the comb lifts the wax up about as easily as fancy wax remover. For a **pristine** deck, follow up by rubbing paint thinner or acetone with a soft cloth.

RAD TIP

Shade Your Board

Don't leave your board facing deck up in the sun for longer than five minutes. Even on a cool day, the sun melts the wax into a nasty mess. Then the wind blows sand into the melted wax and your deck feels like it's wrapped in extra-rough sandpaper.

PLAY SAFE

Surfers take risks every time they splash their boards. Waves sneak up on riders. So do sea critters. Other surfers, spongers, and swimmers can easily mess you up, too. Think ahead. Stay alert and use common sense.

NEVER SURF ALONE

Stick close to your surf buddy. If your buddy heads for the shore, you should also head in—immediately. The two of you need to check on each other all the time.

chapter

THREE

Lifeguards watch the waves for trouble. They rule the beach.
Don't argue with them.

NOW HEAR THIS

You might not be able to see some risks. Cold air and water whipping inside your ear canal every day can cause extra bone growth called **exostosis**, or "surfer's ear." The added bumpy bone shrinks the canal opening, trapping bacteria. Infections blossom.

Prevent the pain. Wear surfers' earplugs that vent if you wipe out. Pull up a hood so your ears stay warm and dry.

Other health **hazards**, including toxic chemicals and oil spills, come from water pollution. Sinus infections, **hepatitis**, and other diseases lurk in scummy water. Avoid it. Do what you can to keep the oceans clean and beaches open.

STARTER BEACHES

Beginners need their own practice area. Find a quiet beach with knee- or waist-high waves and a sandy bottom. Ask local surfers for places to start.

Even when you find the perfect waves, you may be out of luck. Lifeguards can "blackball" the area and ban stand-up surfing. Don't argue. Save your energy for finding another perfect place to rip.

RAD TIP

Oceanside Safety

Surfers, spongers, and swimmers who play in the ocean live longer, healthier lives by following these basic rules:

- Never panic. The Laws of Physics are on your side—you will float to the surface.
- Surf with a buddy. No exceptions.
- Always face the waves; watch the water before and during your session.
- Don't shield yourself with your board; waves can whack it down hard on you.
- Know the depth and what's on the bottom where the waves break.
- Do not feed the fish, especially sharks. Beach it until bait fish move on.
- Open bleeding wounds? Two words: shark bait. Stay out of the water.
- Thunderstorms cancel water activities. End of discussion.
- Blue lips, shaky muscles, or shivering mean it's time for a break.
- Drink a full bottle of water about 45 minutes before you surf; bring water to the beach to avoid dehydrating.

DUCK AND PADDLE

Paddling sounds easy, but it's really a lot of hard work to make it out past the breaking water to the line-up.

First, drop your pride on the beach. You won't need it. Then walk out as far as you can, about waist deep. Center yourself on your board. Paddle with one arm at a time, just like you practiced in your backyard. Spend some time paddling until you feel balanced on the board.

Push the board's nose under the breaking wave and pop out the other side. Keep paddling! Don't give up. Duck and paddle, duck and paddle. After you're outside, catch your breath before you catch a wave.

CATCH THAT WAVE

When you're ready, practice in the whitewater. (Planing in the open face of the wave happens later, after you swallow your share of saltwater and dial in your basic skills.) Aim for 10 to 20 feet (3.048 to 6.096 m) beyond the breaking waves. Feel the wave rhythm as you float there. Mind your manners in the line-up.

Wait.
Wait.
Wait.

As a solid wave approaches, paddle toward shore until it begins to lift you up. You'll feel the surge, in the same way a baseball feels a surge when a bat smacks it. Now put your dry-land practice into play. Grab the rails. Step into your stance. Prepare to get drilled.

Learn to balance on your stomach and paddle.

Sitting up on your board so you can see the waves will also take practice.

WIPEOUT WISDOM

The wave wins more often than you do, especially at first. Everyone wipes out. So prepare to get pounded. When you fall, take a deep breath. Try to keep your body on the up-side of the board, with the board between you and the beach.

Bring your arms up to guard your noggin, and tuck your chin to your chest. Don't give the wave or your board a target. Close your eyes and calmly wait for the wave to pass by. Then open your eyes to find the surface and scramble up for air.

Keep one hand around your head until you find your board. Nab your board quickly before it pounds you in the next wave. (If it's too late, push the nose down and dive with it under the wave. Don't grab the fins—they bite during the wave thrashing.) Get out of the impact zone. Then paddle back for more!

Going over the falls and landing in the impact zone. Not fun!

Leash It
Always use the surfboard leash, the line attached at the tail. Why? Losing your board stinks. Worse, a loose board can take out another surfer. Strap the leash to your rear foot, usually at the ankle. Practice taking it off, too. And always hang onto your board as if it didn't have a leash. Leashes can break.

A leash should be securely attached to the board and strapped to your ankle.

BETTER BODY, BETTER SURFER

Better surfing starts with better warm-ups. Really. Take ten minutes to warm up and stretch as you watch the waves. Do jumping jacks or swing your arms to pump up your heart rate. This amps the blood flow to your muscles for fewer injuries and better reactions. Stretching all of the major muscles gains **flexibility** and balance, too.

Cross-training also conditions your body for the beating it takes. Swimming, skateboarding, snowboarding, and yoga are top choices. Basic push-ups, sit-ups, lunges, and squats work wonders for your body and your control.

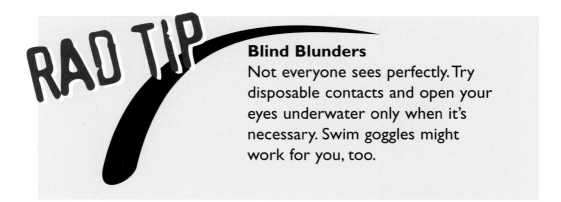

RAD TIP

Blind Blunders
Not everyone sees perfectly. Try disposable contacts and open your eyes underwater only when it's necessary. Swim goggles might work for you, too.

WILD WAVES

Freesurfing recharged the wild and fun spirit of the sport for many surfers. New board designs and high-tech construction materials gave better surfers more control and precise performance, even in smaller waves.

Only advanced surfers should try for the sky. If you're still shaky in the whitewater, forget sticking a 360° (a full spin). Big-air moves take a lot of skill and even more practice.

chapter

FOUR

STICKING TRICKS

Surfers speak their own lingo. A bro (surfer) in California might call waves, body positions, and tricks something totally different than a brah (surfer) in Hawaii. Everything changes, too. Every year, the sport pops up new tricks. A sick, or cool, move today could be dull tomorrow. In the 1930s, a bottom turn blew people away. Now it's a bust-out Barney-oops that wows fans.

Surfing tricks build up from basic moves. Generally, keep your knees bent to absorb impact. A low, crouched position gives you more control over the board and better balance, too. Use balance and pressure to change your direction. Pressure on your toe-side, where your toes point out, curves the board away from you. Pressure heel-side creates an inward curve.

RAD TRICK: REVERSE
Skill Level: Basic

After you find your groove frontside, what's next? Before you can move on to big-air moves, learn to ride reverse or backside. For a regular foot, a backside means you go left on a wave. This is your left, not the beach crew's left. A goofy foot backside cruises right on a wave.

You double your trick potential by riding with your back to the wave, or wall. So, a "backside air" means launching off a wave with your back to the wall. A frontside move means you face the wall.

Frontside means you ride facing the wave.

Backside means you ride with your back to the wave.

RADTRICK: CUTBACK

Skill Level: Basic to Intermediate

You're still not ready for the Green Room, or riding the tube of a wave. After you learn to ride frontside and backside, take command of your moves with **cutbacks**. This sharp turn lets you change your "cut" on the wave toward or away from the peak. Variations include a cutback off the lip, a backside cutback, and a backside cutback off the lip.

A more advanced move, roundhouse cutbacks drop and climb the wave in a fluid "S" line. Avoid herky-jerky roundhouse cuttys. Drop from high on the wave, keeping your knees bent and your body low. Gain speed—lots of speed. Stay on the rail for a faster, cleaner line (but don't dig the rail or welcome to Biff City!).

Make a bottom turn when you reach the flats. Bank hard in the trough, brushing your hand in the water for added style and a sharper turn. When your heel-side rail holds the line, pump hard. Aim for the corner of the falling lip. Let the foam's force swing the nose back. Whoo-yah!

You need speed to climb the wave for a cutback.

Keep your knees bent and your body low as you reach the peak.

Stay on the rail as you curve back down.

RADTRICK: FLOATER

Skill Level: Basic to Intermediate

Like grinders in the half-pipe, floaters skim the top of the wave. Surfers swoop up to the break or just behind the crumble point. You ride along at the peak, maybe even dipping into the "soup" on the collapsed backside of the lip. Then you drop back down the wave face. Keep your stance low and wide.

Floaters look like skateboarding grinds as the surfer skims the wave.

RADTRICK: AERIAL RE-ENTRY

Skill Level: Intermediate to Advanced

Aerials work better on beachbreaks and choppy surf, because the wall bends like a bowl. A steep bowl makes the best ramp.

Drop down fast on the face. Then cut back up the middle of the wave. Pump hard for speed. Aim for the corner of the wave where the foam just starts to dribble down the face. Shift your weight back slightly to lift the nose up. The broken water surges under the nose, springing your launch higher off the lip.

To rotate back for your re-entry, turn your head where you want to drop back in. Keep your knees bent with a wide stance. Drop back in tail first like an airplane for a smooth landing.

RADTRICK: FRONTSIDE DOUBLE-GRAB AIR

Skill Level: Advanced

Pump your board for serious speed. When you find your launch lip, prep your stance by moving forward. Make a bottom turn to the lip. As you fly off, tuck to grab both rails. Don't let go until you reach your highest point. Then push your legs down, but keep your knees loose to take the impact. Land and take it out with a floater.

A double-grab air, with both hands on the rails, shows plenty of style.

Flow Riders on man-made waves pull tricks like skateboarders do.

INLAND SURFING

Surfing expanded beyond the ocean in the 1990s with flowboarding. Tom Lochtefeld invented the Flow Rider to mimic ocean waves. A 10-foot (3.048-m) barrel wave, called Bruticus Maximus, spews out at 25 miles (40.2 km) per hour from four jet pumps. No sharks. No pollution. No **rogue** waves.

Like a skateboard half-pipe, the wave doesn't really change. Riders on special flowboards easily link moves. They borrow a lot of skateboarding tricks, too.

GREAT LAKES FANATICS

For hard-core surfers, the Great Lakes promise extreme surfing with few crowds. The best waves run from September to November. A hearty nor'easter in November can kick up 30-foot (9.14-m) waves on Lake Superior. Instead of sharks, these surfers watch for ice.

Of course, Great Lakes surfers wear wetsuits for warmth. Freshwater isn't as buoyant as saltwater; wetsuits also add flotation. Sessions often last less than 30 minutes because of the cold and because the waves often come with five-second periods—not the leisurely 12-second periods common on the ocean. Paddling takes focus and strength. Ripping it up in a cove of your own makes it worthwhile.

BIG-WAVE ASSAULTS

Big-wave riders once flocked to Hawaii's Banzai Pipeline for huge challenges. But the Oahu high surf isn't enough for some stick-riders. Elite tow-in surfers catch a ride by boat or personal watercraft into monster-wave zones far away from the beach. Some drop in by helicopter. They ride big guns with foot straps to tame rogues topping 30 feet (9.14 m).

Three decades after California became the hot spot for surfing, serious surfers there discovered a big-wave source in their backyard. Maverick's, looming off central California's coast, tests the best. It kills, too. Cold and unforgiving, this radical ride is the ultimate in big-wave surfing.

Surfers have always loved the tube ride of the Pipeline.

CHAMPION CHARGERS

Surfing well is difficult. Finding a contest is easy. In America, hundreds of contests challenge nearly 10,000 surfers every year. The U.S. Open of Surfing attracts more than 700 riders alone.

The United States Surfing Federation, formed in 1980, coordinates U.S. surfing competitions and emphasizes judging standards. A member of the International Surfing Association (ISA), the USSF also chooses the United States National Surfing Team for international competitions.

chapter

FIVE

THE ELITE OF THE ELITE

Big-name and big-buck contests whittle down the pack to a few elite surfers. The Professional Surfing Tour of America (PSTA) series, the Surfing Magazine Airshow Series (SMAS), and the Vans Triple Crown of Surfing competitions include World Qualifying Series (WQS) and World Championship Tour (WCT) events.

Every year, only 42 men and 14 women surfers from all over the world compete for the World Championship. The Association of Surfing Professionals (ASP), which **sanctions** the competitions, names pro surfers to its Top 44—the most elite of the elite.

JUDGING JUDGES

Judges use their surfing knowledge, experience, and a lot of personal opinion to award points to surfers. Riders compete in heats, catching a certain maximum number of waves in each heat. Usually, the surfer skilled (and lucky) enough to spot the best wave can pull the best moves. The rider with the most points wins.

Judges watch each surfer for a strong takeoff position, powerful turns, smooth movements, speed, and ride **duration**. The number of tricks is not as important as how well the tricks are executed—at least, according to the judges' guidebook.

Still, judging is **subjective**. Do your best. Have fun.

RAD TIP

No Olympic Surfers—Yet
The International Olympic Committee (IOC) decides which sports compete in the Olympic programs. ISA leads the global movement to include surfing in the Olympics. More than 48 countries belong to ISA. They promote bodysurfing, bodyboarding, and surfing all over the world.

Winning a surfing competition takes a lot of practice, skill, and luck.

STARS IN THE SURF

Today's surfing stars like Sunny Garcia, Mikala Jones, Andy Irons, Kelly Slater, the Hobgood brothers, Rob Machado, Derek Ho, and Tom Carroll (and too many more to name) continue to raise the standards for competitions.

Right behind them, Jensen Callaway (called El Kelito, meaning the little Kelly) and Eric Geiselman promise to keep the pressure up.

But it's not just guys. **Wahine**, the Hawaiian word for girls, rip it up on gnarly curls, too. Serena Brooke, Keala Kennelly, Rochelle Ballard, Layne Beachley, and Megan Abubo each rock with unique style.

THE ALL-TIME ROYALTY

The founder of modern surfing first gained fame as an Olympic swimmer. Hawaiian Duke Paoa Kahanamoku won three gold medals, starting with a record-breaking 100-yard (91.44 m) freestyle win at the 1912 event in Stockholm, Sweden. He represented the U.S. for 20 years in Olympic events.

Duke trained by surfing the big waves off Oahu and other islands. He feared nothing in the water. People gathered on the beach to watch him command his 114-pound (51.7- kg), 16-foot (4.88-m) longboard. In 1917, he rode a bluebird, a mammoth wave, for about half a mile. He used his fame to share his love for surfing with the world.

FAN FOCUS

Name: Vincent "Sunny" Garcia
Born: January 14, 1970
Home: Kauai, Hawaii
Started Competing: 1986
Vans Triple Crown of Surfing Titles:
    Five-time champion
World Championship Tour Title: 2000

Some of surfing's biggest fans never get wet. They play very realistic video and computer games. They watch videos of their favorite riders. They watch the contests on network and cable TV. The non-stop action and sunny beach images draw viewers and fans to EXPN every year for the Summer X Games.

Museums around the world also showcase the sport's impact on culture and competition. The California Surf Museum in Oceanside opened in 1986 and presents different displays of old equipment and photographs every six months. About 20,000 people visit the museum each year.

Also in California, The International Surfing Museum anchors the Huntington Beach Surfing Walk of Fame. A granite stone honors each inductee, including Duke Kahanamoku. Huntington Beach earned the title "Surf City, USA" because more people surf there than any other beach on the West Coast.

FURTHER READING

Maverick's: The Story of Big-wave Surfing by Matt Warshaw. Chronicle Books, San Francisco, 2000.

Men Who Ride Mountains by Peter Dixon. The Lyons Press, New York, 2001.

The Ultimate Guide to Surfing by Jay Moriarity and Chris Gallagher. The Lyons Press, New York, 2001.

WEBSITES TO VISIT

www.surfermag.com
www.surfingthemag.com
www.surfinggirl.com
www.transworldsurf.com
www.expn.com
www.ExtremeSports.com
www.vans.com
www.surfinfo.com
www.ussurf.org
www.surfingamerica.org

GLOSSARY

aerials (air ee alz) — tricks or moves performed in the air

buoyancy (BOY an see) — the power to float or rise in water

cutbacks (KUT baks) — in surfing, sharp turns toward or away from the wave peak

duration (doo RAY shun) — the time period that something continues

exostosis (ek so STOH sis) — bony growth on a bone or tooth; it causes "surfer's ear"

flexibility (FLEK sah BILL uh tee) — ability to bend and stretch

hazards (HAZ ardz) — risks or dangers

hepatitis (hep ah TIH tis) — a liver illness caused by virus or poison

momentum (moh MEN tum) — forward or ongoing movement

neoprene (NEE oh preen) — a lightweight, manufactured rubber used in wetsuits and other products

physics (FIZ iks) — the science of matter, energy, motion, and force

Polynesians (pol eh NEE zhunz) — people of the Pacific islands from Hawaii to New Zealand

posers (POH zurz) — people who act like they know a lot about a sport or topic, but know very little; also called spasts

pristine (PRIS teen) — pure or original condition

riptide (RIP tihd) — a water current that runs against the normal current; also called an undertow

rogue (ROHG) — unpredictable or unusual; mean or savage

sanctions (SANGK shunz) — to make, approve, or check the rules

stance (STANSE) — a proper body position for control and safety

subjective (sub JEK tiv) — not based on fact; personal opinion, mood, or attitude

traction (TRAK shun) — the ability of a foot or wheel to grip the terrain or surface

trough (TROFF) — in surfing, the lowest part of the wave

wahine (wa HEE nee) — Hawaiian and Polynesian word for girls or young women

INDEX

ABOUT THE AUTHOR

Tracy Nelson Maurer specializes in nonfiction and business writing. Her most recently published children's books include the *Radsports I* series, also from Rourke Publishing LLC. She lives with her husband Mike and two children in Superior, Wisconsin.